D0721750

SEW SOMETHING SPECIAL

Sewing with Handwoven Fabrics

Linda Kubik Curtis
Illustrations by Ruth Voshell

Publishing services provided by:  Well Dressed
Publications
5720 Park Manor Drive
San Jose, CA 95118
(408) 265-7074

❧

This book is dedicated
to all my students, who encouraged
(and badgered) me to write it.

❧

About the Author

Linda Kubik Curtis is a handweaver who makes her home in rural Eastern Washington. Linda has been weaving for the past twelve years and sewing forever! She holds a degree in Clothing, Textiles and Art from the University of Washington. Textiles and fiber have always been her passion and she enjoys sharing her enthusiasm and knowledge in her workshops and seminars.

Linda exhibits and sells throughout North America and has been invited to submit entries to juried competitions. She is currently marketing distinctive handwoven fabrics to home-sewers through her weaving studio, Twill & Tuck. She's available for workshops and seminars.

About This Book

Sew Something Special grew out of a need for handling specialty fabrics, particularly handwoven fabric. This book is for weavers and sewers alike. I have tried to address two audiences, those who are not familiar with weaving and working with handwoven fabric and weavers who are not familiar or comfortable with sewing.

I've had a passion for fibers and textiles all my life, specifically for the unusual and out-of-the ordinary. Textiles should not only look good, but feel good. Whether crisp, firm, sheer or bulky, good textiles should provide a sensual delight in working with them. That is what I attempt to provide with my fabrics.

After you have read this book you should feel comfortable working with handwoven and specialty fabrics.

In the Sew It Up section, I have tried to explain sewing terms and methods for any fabric first, and then to concentrate on where the method changes for handwovens. I want to make sure everyone is able to sew successfully with these gorgeous fabrics!

Linda

Introduction

Specialty fabrics should not intimidate the home-sewer. For hundreds of years, all fabrics were handwoven and sewn by hand. Power looms were not used until the Industrial Revolution and the sewing machine was not invented until the middle of the 19th century. Ready-to-wear is a recent innovation in the clothing history.

Table of Contents

Fabrics

A Short Course on Weaving

Most fabric is an interlacement of threads and fibers. These can be felted, knitted, crocheted or woven. I am a handweaver. I weave fabric for clothing using a traditional human powered loom.

Looms are like cars with many makes and models to choose from. Your choice depends on your likes and your budget. I am often asked by non-weavers how long it takes to weave one yard. I can't say how long it takes as it varies with the materials used and sometimes the weather. I do know it takes at least 5 hours to prepare a warp (lengthwise threads) and dress the loom (putting each thread through its own heddle eye, similar to threading a sewing machine needle 700 times).

Weave Types

There are many different types of weave structures, the most common being twills, ribs, satin and overshots. All of these weave structures have a floating thread, some quite long, which may affect the durability of the piece. They are usually denser, heavier fabrics than plain weaves, with more threads per square inch. The weave structure affects the hand and drape of the fabric. Choose a handwoven fabric for the color, hand and drape you want for a particular garment.

Plain Weave

My favorite weave structure is plain weave. This is one weft or filling thread (the crosswise thread) going over, then under each warp (the grain or length). Colors and textures can become lost in complicated weave structures. More complicated weave structures have many uses and we most often see them in home furnishings. Most commercial fabrics, whether printed or yarn dyed use simple weave structures, either plain weave or twill variations.

My fabrics are known for their color and texture, sometimes incorporating ribbons and metallics with several different colored yarns. There are always some hand-dyed yarns included to give a flow of movement and surprise not found in commercial fabrics.

My fabrics generally have the color or pattern woven on the warp of the fabric. This is somewhat different from other handwoven fabrics you will find; as many others have their color or pattern woven on the weft. By having the pattern on the warp, I can provide a stable yet drapable fashion fabric with a good hand. The fabric will tailor well if it's wool and withstand both washer and dryer if it's cotton. A stable fabric is firm enough not to poke your finger through, but not so stiff it can be mistaken for poster board.

A fabric woven with its pattern on the weft will generally result in the pattern being horizontal around the body, and at times this is not a look that you may want. Change the garment grainline to the crossgrain if you really love the fabric.

Handwoven fabric is not finished until it is "fulled". Fulling is simply washing the fabric to set the weave structure and allowing the yarns to relax and bloom. All my handwovens are sold preshrunk and ready to cut. Commercially woven wool can also benefit from fulling. The "hand" or the feel of the fabric can change dramatically, so you may want to test a sample first.

What to look for in quality handwoven fabric:

- Is it structurally durable?
  - Can you poke a finger through it?
  - Is it too stiff to mold around the body easily?
- Is the fabric the right weight for the project you're making?
- Is raveling a problem?
- Is the fabric uniformly woven?

Different Fiber Choices

Handwoven fabrics will most often be wool, silk, cotton or a combination of fibers. A predominantly wool fabric should be treated like a commercially woven wool fabric. Handwoven silks and cottons are generally heavier than commercial yardage due to the size of yarns available to handweavers. Good handwoven cotton will still have the care and desirability of a good quality commercial fabric, i.e., easily laundered, comfortable, and hard wearing.

When the fabric is a blend of fibers, treat it as you would the most fragile component, such as wool in a wool/cotton fabric. Handweavers love to incorporate novelty yarns and fibers, such as ribbons and metallics. These should not change the hand or drape or care of the fabric.

HINT

Hold the fabric to the light and look for evenness and uniformity in the crosswise threads. Put both cut edges together, are they the same width? Do the same for the length. Are plaid blocks or patterns the same shape and size? Can you see any glaring flaws such as skipped threads or holes?

Fabric Types

Handwoven fabrics usually have no right or wrong side. Most plain weaves and twills are reversible. Unless there is a definite pattern, don't worry about right and wrong side.

Two types of handwovens require special handling:

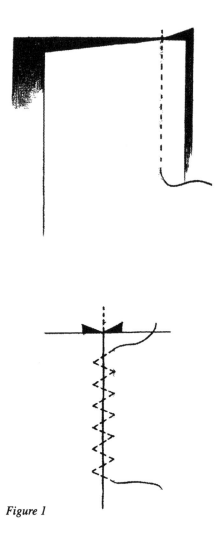

Chenille
Chenille is a woven yarn consisting of many threads held together with binder yarns to create a tufted look. It has a soft, fuzzy hand and appearance.

Chenille fabrics require careful finishing. Even if the garment is to be lined, it is a good idea to finish the seam edges to prevent raveling during construction. To keep the seams flat, stitch, press, then topstitch the seams using a three-step zigzag. (see Figure 1) This will not be noticeable in the finished garment and is particularly important where seams are closely graded, such as collars and necklines.

Figure 1

When sewing chenille to a commercial fabric, put the chenille against the feed dogs so the feed dogs can ease the chenille to the more stable fabric.

Chenille can be cotton, rayon, acrylic or any combination of these. They all shrink differently. Rayon and acrylic will become shiny with over-pressing and acrylic may melt.

Mohair
Mohair comes from the angora goat. It is a long, lustrous fiber that takes dye well and is often used in novelty and bouclé yarns to add wonderful texture. Mohair is usually quite hard wearing but gets fuzzy with wear. Brushed mohair yarn is spun fuzzy.

Handwoven fabrics with mohair yarns will have a fuzzier side that can be brushed for more loft.

Mohair is usually used as a weft (crosswise) yarn. The weave structure is generally more open because if too closely woven, the fabric will be too stiff and definitely too hot for garments. Fabrics of 40-50% mohair can be warm, yet lightweight. Fuzzy mohair felts somewhat during fulling making a virtually ravel-free fabric.

Handwovens: The Challenge

Sewing with handwoven fabric is an exercise in fabric manipulation rather than detailed pattern sewing. The more complicated the fabric, the simpler the pattern should be. Let the fabric show itself off.

Preshrinking

Preshrink the fabric in the manner you wish to care for the finished garment. If you want to machine wash and dry cottons, run the fabric through a wash and dry cycle at the same temperature the finished garment will be cared for. Wool can be professionally steamed. My choice is to do it myself by immersing the fabric in a sink full of hot tap water. Do not agitate unless you wish to felt the fabric. This method can be used for commercially woven wool, especially tweeds and will dramatically soften the hand. Silk fabric can also be treated in this manner, but be prepared for some dye bleeding. Silk holds excess dye during the dyeing process and it may take several washings for it to all disappear.

Cutting

When cutting your pattern out, any good pair of sharp dressmakers shears will work well. A rotary cutter may or may not work. Be careful with handmade fabrics that have embellishments woven into the fabric that might cause problems—particularly metal, wood, sequins or glass!

To determine the straight grain, on the crosswise length, pull a thread and cut along the path.

Then, match up the raw edges. Be careful that the crosswise grain does not shift when cutting handwoven fabrics. It is not necessary to cut each piece separately, but if this is your preference, cut one side, then flip the pattern over with the first side still attached so that the pattern is sandwiched between the two layers of fabric. This method also works well for matching plaids and stripes and eliminates the possibility of cutting two left fronts!

Patterns

Loom-shaped garments do not flatter nor fit *any* body. Always use a pattern to give you opportunities to mold the fabric around your body. Your body is *not* flat, like a piece of fabric—it is three-dimensional.

Good basic patterns and lines can be found in most of the Stretch & Sew patterns. My current other favorites are Neue Mode and Lois Ericson's patterns. Neue Mode is a German company with European fit and the patterns are multi-size for a better fit.

Tips On Choosing a Pattern

Choose clean, uncluttered lines. This does not mean avoiding princess or raglan lines, but does mean avoiding fussy details like ruffles or peplums.

Determine your body shape. Are you rectangular, round or pear shaped? What are your best features? What do you wish to camouflage? What styles do you feel comfortable in? Try to analyze why. For help, read *Flatter Your Figure* by Jan Larkey.

Always make a muslin test garment to ensure the pattern fits and flatters. Old bath towels are great for a test muslin if your fashion fabric has some body and texture.

Which Patterns Work Best

Some handwoven fabrics have minimal drape, so look for designs that have opportunities to create shape against your body. Princess seams, darts, lapels and set-in or modified raglan sleeves will give you the opportunity to make the garment conform better to your body and make you look wonderful.

Fitting

Never assume you wear a certain size—measure and remeasure. Have a friend help. True measurements are particularly important when using European patterns, as the cut and fit is different than American companies offer. Don't be appalled that you may wear a larger size in a pattern than you would in ready-to-wear. If you measure and cut accordingly, the fit will be better than American patterns or ready-to-wear.

Patterns without seam allowances are sometimes intimidating. Cut out the pattern on your size (with alterations). Fit the paper pattern. If it looks okay, go ahead and cut, remembering to add seam allowances. Adding seam allowances can be simple if you are using a rotary cutter with a seam allowance guide attached. The seam allowance guide is an arm that sticks out from the side of the cutter and can be placed ⅝" from the cutting blade. You place the arm on the stitching line of the pattern, and voila, your blade is properly positioned ⅝" from the stitching line of the garment. You cannot fit a pattern with the seam allowances attached. If this is too scary, trace the pattern on other paper and add seam allowances. If this is still scary, make the seam allowances 1" on the side seams and shoulders. Still scary? Make a test garment.

You may need to alter the bust and back, but remember, you want to focus attention on your face, so the neckline area must fit.

There are lots of books and methods available on alterations so they won't be covered here. My favorite is Nancy Zieman's pivot-and-slide method found in her book, *Fitting Finesse*.

A word about American patterns. . . Even couture patterns are drafted on a standardized American sloper, so you are not getting the designer's fit. Most American pattern companies base their measurements on a B-cup bra. So if you're bigger (or smaller) you need to alter. If you buy a pattern solely by your bust measurement, it may not fit around the neckline unless you are relatively flat chested.

Do as many alterations as possible on the flat pattern before cutting out the garment. Excessive alterations after the garment is cut and sewn will decrease your enjoyment of the garment and the process. Some alterations will be unavoidable, but these should be kept to a minimum. The better you know your body, the more automatic alterations become as you measure and cut the pattern.

What makes or breaks a garment is fit and finishing (this leaves lots of room for error in between). The most exquisite sewing will not camouflage poor fit. Hastily sewn hems and buttons will detract from the finished garment, but a seam that is not perfectly straight will probably never be noticed.

Pattern ease is different than fitting ease! There must be enough room in a normal fitting garment for the body to move. This is called fitting ease. Pattern ease is part of the design. A swing coat or boxy jacket will have design ease as well as fitting ease. Unless you like your clothes skin tight, below are some standards for fitting ease for a close fitting or highly tailored garment (you may want more).

Bust	1-2"
Hips	2+"
Arm	2"

There shouldn't be any fitting ease around the neck unless it is a pullover pattern.

Handwoven fabrics should never be made into skintight garments. There is too much stress on the seams when the garment is too tight. That's not to be interpreted as handwovens cannot be used for fitted garments. Generally tailored is better than trendy for handwoven fabrics.

Laying Out Handwoven Fabric

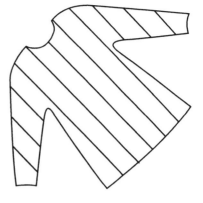

Typically, when laying out a pattern, you are instructed to make sure the grainlines marked on the pattern match exactly with the fabric grainline, because the lengthwise grain of the fabric is usually the strongest. Most patterns are designed to have the stress of the garment on the grainlines. While this rule holds true for handwoven fabrics, you are hereby given permission to break those rules! Grainlines are not sacrosanct. Some spectacular results may result when the grainline is switched to the crossgrain. Some fabrics, such as polyester, demand a crosswise grain.

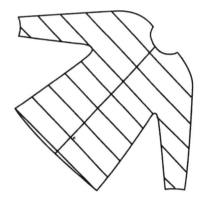

Whether the fabric has definite or subtle stripes, experiment and look what happens when the grainline is rotated and utilized to its advantage. Feel free to mix grainlines, particularly on raglan styles. The result may be more dramatic and slimming.

On some handwoven fabrics, you will find the design has been created in a crosswise direction (perpendicular to the lengthwise grainline). Since it is a handmade creation, you may find that trying to match the design at critical seams (side, sleeve, back, etc.) is impossible. There are options to avoid having to match these design lines. One option is to use a seam finish such as a covered seam. Another option is to use only selected pattern pieces from the handwoven fabric (yokes, fronts, pockets) which will avoid the matching problem.

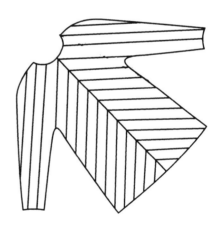

If grainline distortion or sagging is a concern, the whole garment can be stabilized with fusible interfacing. Fuse the whole piece of yardage before cutting or cut the interfacing on the suggested grainline and fuse the garment piece by piece. Make sure you do several test pieces with different types of interfacing to determine the correct one to use. You want to make sure you aren't adding too much stiffness or bulk to your garment.

An Inside Look

Interfacing

Handwoven fabrics will stretch with wearing. For washable, unlined garments, this is not a problem. Simply run them through the washer and dryer. For lined garments it may or may not be a problem, depending on the fabric weave structure. If the fabric is loosely-woven or prone to stretching out of shape, you may need full interfacing throughout the garment to add shape, strength and stability.

To test fabric for excessive stretch, measure it and hang it over a padded hanger for several days. Then remeasure it. More than 1" stretch per yard is excessive. If there is more than 1-2" of stretch, you will need to add interfacing to each and every garment piece. The exception would be a washable, unlined garment. Other options for combating specific stretch sites include interfacing the seat only of pants and skirts, or the knee area of slacks. In these circumstances, the best interfacing would be a knitted fusible that requires high heat and moisture to adhere to the fabric.

Interfacing Types
There are many different types of interfacing. Construction ranges from woven to nonwoven to knitted. Each type may either be a fusible or non-fusible. There are several types of fusible interfacings that require low heat and little moisture for fusing. Some of the new fusibles become sew-ins after construction is complete, such as Touch of Gold™.

Sew-in interfacings may be the same as the garment fabric for lightweight wovens, or batiste, muslin or organza. In all cases, the care and compatibility of the fashion fabric and the interfacing must be the same.

Nonwoven interfacings are flexible and ravel-free with no grainline direction. Unfortunately they are somewhat stiff. You can choose an all-bias, nonwoven interfacing for outerwear. Non-stretch, non-wovens include belt backing and are generally stiff and heavy and are better suited for craft projects than garments.

Coats and tailored garments traditionally use hair canvas for interfacing. Hair canvas should not wrinkle when squashed in your hand. The higher the percentage of goat hair, the better the hair canvas. Speed tailoring eliminates the need for hair canvas and padded hand stitches by using different weights of fusible interfacings layered over each other (see the Speed Tailoring section for more information).

PRESHRINK ALL INTERFACINGS BEFORE USING. This may be done by dipping or steaming. Dip fusible interfacings in hot tap water and drip dry. Do NOT use boiling water on fusibles. Fusible interfacing can also be pressed to eliminate wrinkles using a non-stick pressing cloth next to the resin side or steam as for non-washable linings. Purchasing 5-10 yards at a time and pre-shrinking means there is always some ready to use.

Rotary cutters work well for cutting out fusible interfacings. When you cut interfacing, most often you will use the same grainlines as the garment. However, bias cut garments may have too much sag. For a structured garment cut on the bias, cut the interfacing on the grainline that is at a 90°angle from the garment grainline. This will eliminate any unwanted sagging or bagging.

Read, save and follow the printed instructions that come with your fusible interfacings. Each type of fusible interfacing is different and has a different fusing time and temperature. Test several different types of interfacing on samples of your fashion fabric before you make a final decision. The end result of using a fusible interfacing will be a crisper hand than using a similar weight sew-in interfacing. Fusibles are not a good choice for metallic or napped yardage or anything that is heat- or moisture-sensitive. As a rule, too soft is better than too stiff. When fusing interfacing to your fabric, use a press cloth and follow the recommended instructions. *Press*, do not slide the iron. When all the pieces are fused and dry, turn each piece over and press from the right side, using a press cloth. An old cotton tea towel makes a great press cloth.

After fusing the interfacing, trim off any overhang so the interfacing matches the fabric.

Use fusible fleece as an interfacing to add loft without weight and to give a rounded appearance to purses and pillows. Fusible fleece can be fused to lightweight fabrics such as silk for machine embroidery and appliqué.

Lining

Why line a garment? A lining is an inner garment, which helps protect the shape, prevents cling and stretch, reduces wrinkles, adds body and finishes the garment.

There are several different types of lining material. Commonly polyester and rayon fibers are used, but if you really want to splurge, you can use a lightweight silk, like a good crepe de Chine for your lining. My preference is a rayon lining, such as Ambiance (the brand name for Bemberg™) rayon.

All lining should be preshrunk before you cut it. If the lining requires dry cleaning, you can preshrink it by steaming with your iron. Hold the iron over the lining fabric, steam and let it dry before moving it. Most rayons and all acetates should be preshrunk by steaming as they don't handle washing well and typically go into dry cleanable garments.

The easiest way to line a garment is to pick a pattern that calls for lining and has lining pieces included in the pattern. Make sure the jacket lining has an ease pleat in the back. If there is not a pleat on the pattern, add a 1" pleat (2" total), which can be incorporated into a seam allowance if there is a center back seam. If the jacket does not have a center back seam, place the center back fold line of the lining piece 1" from the edge of the fabric to accommodate the width of the pleat.

If, in the course of making a muslin or test garment of the pattern, you have made alterations, you need to make sure you make the identical alterations on your lining! Once you have made alterations to the pattern and have cut out your fashion fabric, lay the cut out garment on the lining and cut with a rotary cutter.

To keep the lining hem tucked inside the garment, make the lining 2" shorter than the garment. When the fashion fabric side of the garment is hemmed, the unhemmed lining should come to the edge of the finished garment hem.

There are a number of good references already in print for lining methods. Refer to Sandra Betzina's *Power Sewing* or Cecelia Podolak's *Easy Guide to Sewing Jackets*.

Underlining

Underlining is a layer of fabric attached to the fashion fabric and treated as one. It gives shape and support to the outer layer and is most commonly used on unstable or sheer fabrics. It can also add opacity to a sheer lace weave. Underlining fabric should have enough body to support the handwoven without adding bulk.

Reasons for choosing underlining over interfacing:

1. Fusible interfacing may be too heavy.

2. The whole garment needs to be washable.

3. If the garment is to be worn in hot weather and will need to withstand numerous launderings.

4. Wearer is allergic to fabric or fiber.

Underlining is usually only attached at the seam allowances. Carefully place the fashion fabric on the underlining, keeping grainlines parallel, as it is extremely easy to distort the grainline. Pin-baste or hand-baste in place. Sew or serge the seam allowance for an edge finish and treat the layer of fashion fabric and underlining as one from this point on. When serging, it is imperative that the fashion fabric be placed against the feed dogs. If your serger has a differential feed, adjust it for slight gathering to counteract the stretch of the handwoven fabric. If the garment is to be lined, the edges can be straight stitched rather than serged, $\frac{1}{2}$" from the edge.

If the garment is to be underlined, every piece, including facings, collars and pockets, must also be underlined.

If the handwoven fabric was cut off-grain, it will show up when the underlining is attached. Straighten the grainline(s) by trimming before serging the edges together. Whatever you do, do not use a zigzag as an edge finish—this will further distort the grain.

The underlining can be machine quilted to the garment piece. Great care must be taken not to stretch the pieces out of alignment during quilting. Quilting is easier with the fashion fabric against the feed dogs. When you quilt the underlining to the fashion fabric, your quilting design becomes part of the fashion fabric design and will show to the world. This could be an opportunity for embellishing your fabric. Keep in mind when you quilt the underlining to the fashion fabric the fabric becomes stiffer, so it's a good idea to do a larger sample of a quilted underlining to see if you like the effect on your fabric.

Coco Chanel developed a technique for her suits that uses features of both lining and underlining. Chanel suits have no interfacing. She often incorporated the lining into the decorative edge. The fashion fabric was cut out and placed on the lining, machine quilted to the lining, but not quilted through the seam allowances. The lining was then cut to the shape of the garment piece. The fashion fabric was then stitched together by machine while the lining was stitched together by hand. If the lining fabric was to be incorporated in the edge finish trim, either with braid or piping, it was cut longer around the edges.

Interlining

Interlining is a thermal layer. The interlining fabric can be as diverse as flannel, Thinsulate™ or lambswool. The interlining fabric is treated as an underlining for either the garment or the lining.

Shoulder Pad Alternatives

Fusible fleece can be used to make your own shoulder pads by layering smaller shapes on larger ones. If you hate shoulder pads, but feel your garment needs some shaping, fuse the fleece right on the handwoven fabric (remember to test first). Extended shoulders can be built up and extended by layering fusible fleece right on the fabric.

Fuse the area in question, add one or two additional smaller layers as needed. Fuse the whole area with a final piece, either slightly inside or outside the original area. This technique works well for vests and extended shoulders (see Figure 2).

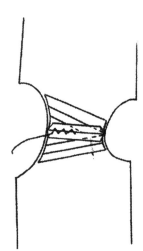

Figure 2

Pressing

You must press every seam as you sew to avoid that "loving hands, made-at-home" look.

Ironing is sliding the iron back and forth, pressing is an up and down motion accomplished by picking up the iron and setting it down in a different place. Ironing can distort the fabric shape, so always press.

Press each stitching line, before pressing the seam allowances open. This helps to flatten the seam for less show-through and crisper looking seams.

Heavy or bulky fabrics may need to have the seams "killed". To kill a seam, the seam allowance only is misted or daubed with water (or use a damp press cloth). Press only the seam allowance using additional pressure. Dry by pounding with a clapper. This flattens only the seam allowance.

The armscye is never killed and usually only pressed in the underarm area. The sleeve cap can be steamed and gently finger pressed towards the sleeve.

Facings and collars also need to be pressed as stitched, pressed open, graded and then and only then, rolled for the final pressing. Always use a press cloth when pressing on the right side of the garment. Allow the fabric to dry before moving it or it may stretch out of shape. Curved shapes should be pressed over a tailor's ham.

Flattening heavy or bulky fabrics can sometimes be a problem. Use a clapper and a wood surface (cheese block). Steam the seam and then pound with the flat side of the clapper on a wood surface until dry. Repeat if necessary. This will produce a crisp edge. The amount of steam and pounding will vary with fabrics, so experiment.

If the seam is pressed flat, it is much easier to grade and either clip or notch if needed. To clip a seam, cut the seam allowance perpendicular to the stitching line; cut right to the stitching. To notch a seam, cut a small wedge shape from the seam allowance, with the pointed end of the wedge touching the stitching line. Clip outside curves, notch inside curves.

Lining seams should be pressed flat and then to one side. The shoulder and side seams are pressed to the back. The only exception is the armscye. This can be pressed as stitched and then gently steamed and finger-pressed towards the sleeve.

Reflective ironing board covers are great for ironing but not for pressing. They do not allow crisp flat seams during the construction process, as heat and moisture bounce back into the fabric making it hard to dry. A layer or two of old wool blanket with a cotton cover provides the best surface. A large, flat surface can be produced easily this way.

Grading

Grading means trimming seam allowances to different widths to eliminate bulk and allowing the garment to fall as designed. Grading is done after pressing. The seam allowance to the outside or top side of the garment should always be longer. After grading, press again.

Trim ¼ - ⅜" off the seam allowance on the top or outer layer. The under layer should be trimmed so that the remaining seam allowance is smaller. The thicker the fabric, the more important it is to kill and grade seam allowances.

Grading seam allowances is just as important with handwoven fabrics as it is with commercially woven fabrics. Properly interfaced and understitched, the seam will not unravel or pull out. With fusible interfacing to the edge, don't worry about the fabric unraveling.

When grading your seams, there are a few tricks to making your finished garment look sharp and professional. Clip the seam over the seam allowances on the diagonal to further reduce bulk. In the lapel area, trim the coat seam narrower than the lapel to the roll line or button-hole. Then the facing is trimmed closer than the coat seam. Necklines and undercollars should be understitched to the facing after grading and pressing. This acts as a reinforcement as well as keeping the facing rolled under.

Armscye seams are never graded, but they are trimmed under the arm. The crotch seams in pants are never graded, but are trimmed just through the bottom of the crotch area.

Sewing It Up

Equipment

These are what I consider sewing essentials:

Sewing machine that makes buttonholes and does the blindhem stitch. A walking foot is helpful for stretchable and loosely-woven fabrics.

Serger or overlock machine for finishing seams. The techniques taught in my workshops and seminars do not require a serger, but personally I wouldn't be without one.

Wooden tailor's clapper to flatten seams.

Tailor's ham with sawdust stuffing for pressing curves.

Appliqué scissors with bent handles and a large lip on one side (these look like a deformed version of surgical scissors). They are traditionally used for close trimming on appliqués. I use them to eliminate the chance of nicking a hole in the handwoven fabric when grading.

Sharp shears with 8" or longer blades and a bent handle. Use one pair on natural fibers only; use a second pair for synthetic fibers.

Small scissors for clipping and trimming.

Sharp sewing machine needles (commonly referred to at H-J needles).

Twill tape for stabilizing shoulder seams of all handwoven garments.

Long pins with brightly colored large heads so they don't get lost in the fabric.

Sturdy ironing board or surface with a non-reflecting cotton cover over a wool pad or blanket.

Steam iron

Needles

Needles are critical to any sewn garment. If your needle is dull, chipped, bent or has a burr, your sewing will have skipped, uneven or wavy stitches. After your initial investment on a sewing machine, hundreds of dollars on fabric, yarns and weaving time, don't get cheap with needles! Sewing machine needles should be changed at least for every two garments.

The best needle for handwoven fabric is an 90/14 and is a H-J—sharp or denim needle.

Needle Notes
All needles come with a number and letter. Below is a quick reference.

The number is the size or thickness. The first number is the European size and the second number is American. The larger the number, the bigger the needle.

Size	Use
65/9	sheers
70/10	lightweight fabric
80/12	best all purpose for wovens and knits
90/14	jeans, corduroy, lightweight upholstery, medium-weight handwovens
100/16	upholstery, jeans, heavy handwovens
110/18	you are purposely creating a hole!

Needles now come in not only different sizes, but shapes as well. The letter specifies the point or tip and shape.

Designation	Use
H	universal, not a sharp, not a ball-point, barely rounded at the tip with a scarf
H-S	use with stretch fabrics, including UltraSuede®
SUK	ball-point, use on Spandex or stretch fabrics
H-J	sharps, or denim needles THIS IS THE ONE FOR HANDWOVENS
NTW	real leather or suede
Metafil	metallic threads
Quilting	going through multiple layers
Double and Triple needles	knits and multiple rows of topstitching
W	creating a purposeful hole, great for heirloom sewing, but not applicable for handwovens
ZWIHO	double needle and wing combination, used for heirloom sewing
N	extra-large eye, good for topstitching or Woolly Nylon

Thread

Good quality thread is uniform and has flexibility and strength. Polyester is best for seams that may have stress, such as knits and all-weather garments and leather. I believe Metrosene and Gutermann are the best brands of polyester thread available on the market today. A good polyester thread out performs the common cotton wrapped polyester threads. Cotton-wrapped polyester combines the worst qualities of both and is not recommended for any garment sewing. Do not use polyester thread on silk unless you are trying to create a puckered seam effect.

For sewing on all handwoven fabrics, 100% cotton is the best. It is more flexible than polyester and produces smoother seams. It has a soft hand and dyes well. Remember, the finer the thread, the smaller the needle. A good brand is Mettler.

Silk thread is for hand sewing only. It is so strong it may cut the fabric or tear a hole in handwoven fabric. A good quality cotton thread works best on silk fabrics.

Texturized nylon thread is great for sergers. It comes in solid and variegated colors. One brand name is Woolly Nylon. Woolly Nylon used to be recommended for the seam finish on all handwovens. I do not particularly like it. A four-thread overlock stitch with cotton thread works just as well.

Monofilament nylon thread bears no resemblance to the old fishline-like transparent thread. This can be used on both sewing machine and sergers. For nearly invisible sewing, try it both in the needle and in the bobbin. Monofilament is a good choice when sewing on patch pockets or to invisibly apply trim on your handwoven garment.

Rayon thread sometimes has more sheen than silk. It is used for machine embroidery, topstitching and decorative sewing. It comes in 30- and 40-weight and pearl. The pearl works well in the upper looper of a serger. I particularly like variegated rayon for decorative stitches, either alone or over a novelty yarn.

Metallics are the latest fashion craze. Machine quilting with metallic thread can be stunning. They come in a variety of colors including gold and silver. All brands are different so experiment. Use a large needle (14-18), sewing slowly, or try the new Metafil needles that do not shred metallic thread. YLI has a thin metallic thread that works equally well in sewing machines or sergers.

Candlelight is YLI's heavy metallic thread. It's great in the upper serger looper, can be used in the bobbin of a sewing machine and is strong enough to weave with. Decorative designs are easy to achieve by couching this to the fabric.

Ribbon Floss™ comes in a myriad of colors and is great for accent. Floss used in the upper looper of a serger is quite attractive. If you want to use it with a regular sewing machine, wind it on the bobbin and sew faceside down. Ribbon Floss™ now comes in metallics.

Weaving yarns can be used in the upper looper of your serger. You need to experiment and may have to bypass the tension device.

Pearl rayon, heavy metallic thread and Ribbon Floss™ make a nice seam finish by themselves when used in the serger's upper looper. Set your machine for a wide, three-thread flatlock and use complimentary colors in the lower looper. This may be used alone for an edge finish or turned under and topstitched.

Puckered seams are often due to the bobbin thread being wound too tightly or stretched during winding. It then relaxes and shrinks causing seam puckering. The best way to prevent this is to be careful when winding the bobbin. Always use a slow, consistent speed when winding. If you have a manual winder (one where you take the bobbin out of its case and attach it to a spindle on you machine), make sure the thread spool doesn't dance on the thread holder. If the spool is free floating, you can lightly place your finger on top of the spool to keep it stable.

Seams

When sewing on handwoven fabrics, experiment with needles, thread and different sewing machine feet to get the best result. Unless I specify otherwise, never use a zigzag stitch to sew or finish a seam. The zigzag stitch stretches the fabric and produces a "lettuce" edge effect.

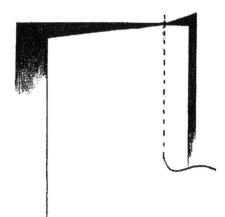

Plain Seam

Handwoven fabrics will typically require a larger size needle and longer stitch length than anticipated. The heavier the fabric, the longer the stitch length. What would appear to be basting on thin, commercially-woven cottons, won't appear so on handwoven fabric.

As you sew a seam, the top layer of fabric is being pushed forward by the friction of the pressure foot, while the bottom layer of fabric is being pushed backward by the action of the feed dogs. To counteract this, use a walking or dual-feed foot. This is a special foot designed to keep both layers of fabric feeding at the same rate. Placing the handwoven fabric against the feed dogs, when sewing commercial fabric lining and handwovens together will also counteract this problem.

You may be tempted to serge a seam. Remember, a serged seam does not usually wear well. After a few washings, the woven threads develop holes unless it is a very dense fabric. If the fabric is heavy or felted, there are options more attractive than a serged seam.

Understitching
Understitching is used to hold seam allowances to an unseen part of a garment. This controls and holds the under piece from creeping out where it doesn't belong. Look for understitching on an undercollar or on facings that lie against the body. Understitching is a construction element rather than a design detail.

To understitch, press the graded seam allowances together toward the part of the garment that doesn't show. Then, from the unseen side, stitch the two seam allowances to the garment, $\frac{1}{8}$" to $\frac{1}{4}$" from the seam.

Topstitching

Topstitching is a decorative line of stitching on the garment outside. It is a design detail and can be used as an accent or can merely be decorative. Topstitching must be done very accurately, as the stitches are large and pronounced. Avoid the "loving hands, made-at-home" look by studying better ready-to-wear for topstitching placement.

You can use a number of different techniques that will help make your topstitching as accurate at possible. There are accessory feet for your machine to help: an edgestitching foot, a straight stitch foot, or a regular foot with an adjustable guide bar.

There are also notions available that will help with topstitching accuracy: a clear topstitching guide, or special adhesive tape that will not leave any residue.

To make your topstitching decorative, you can use different colors or weights of thread, you can use two strands of the thread you used in the garment construction, or you can use one of the many novelty threads available. These threads are used in the needle only.

Make sure that you do a test sample to ensure that you have not only the right stitch length (longer than normal length for bulky fabrics) but also that you are using the correct needle. This may be the time to try a special topstitching needle.

Topstitching is not a substitute for understitching.

Seam Finishes

If the garment is to be lined, there is usually no need for a seam finish as the lining will protect the seam (the exception being chenille fabrics). A four-thread serged edge combined with a plain seam works well for unlined firmly-woven, machine-washable and dryable garments. Experiment with some other finishes which can be used as a decorative addition or as a camouflage for those impossible-to-match designs.

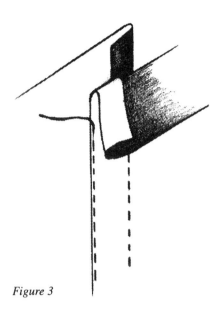

Clean Finish Seam – version 1

A clean finished seam has no right or wrong side, but does require a larger seam allowance. Turn over and press a ½" allowance. Press one underneath so that wrong sides are together. Press the other side with right sides together. Insert one behind the other or butt them together and topstitch each edge. (see Figure 3)

Figure 3

Clean Finish Seam – version 2

This clean finished seam is particularly suitable for unlined, cotton handwoven garments. After sewing a plain seam, press open. Turn under the edges of the seam allowance and topstitch along the edge. This technique can be used either inside or outside the garment. (see Figure 4)

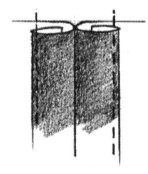

Figure 4

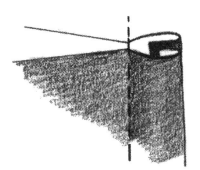

Figure 5

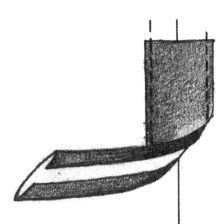

Figure 6

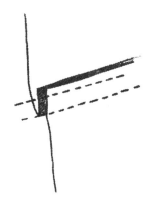

Figure 7

Plain French Seam

A plain French seam works well for lightweight handwovens because it is a seam within a seam. The wrong sides are placed together, a small (¼") seam is sewn. The fabric is then turned right sides together and another seam (⅜" or more) is sewn, enclosing the first seam. (see Figure 5)

Covered Seam

A covered seam is one that has decorative fabric placed over the plain stitched seam allowance. This is similar to the trim on tuxedo pants and can be either on the garment inside or outside. Fold under the edges on the bias trim and topstitch in place. (see Figure 6) For a decorative effect, substitute a fancy braid for the trim fabric.

Mock Flat Fell

A true flat fell seam is usually too bulky for handwoven fabrics, but a mock flat fell seam can be used successfully. (see Figure 7)

- Sew a plain seam and press both seam allowances to one side.

- Topstitch ¼" from the seamline.

- Seam allowances can also be fringed to the outside to become a decorative accent.

Hong Kong Finish

The Hong Kong finish has been used by tailors for years on unlined menswear. This is a very nice finish on unlined garments, however, it is time consuming. Bias strips, usually of light-weight fabric such as China silk or organza, are sewn to the right edges of each seam allowance. (See figure 8, reference point A) They are then rolled over the raw edge and stitched down, either by hand or machine stitching in the ditch. (See figure 8, reference point B) Any excess bias strip on the back side is then trimmed close to the stitching line.

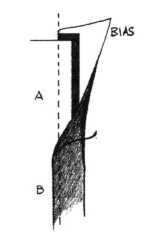

Figure 8

Double Bias Binding

A double bias binding is similar to the Hong Kong finish but the bias strip is doubled. It is then applied like a Hong Kong finish. This can be used around collars and pockets and provides a simple, yet effective edge finish. The binding can also be stuffed or corded for a raised edge. (see Figure 9)

Figure 9

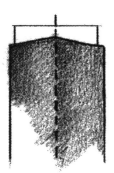

Figure 10

Figure 11

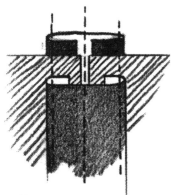

Figure 12

Bound Seam

For heavy fabric or handmade felt, a bound seam is appropriate. Use commercial fabric trim or UltraSuede® in a matching or complimentary color. The binding width can vary with the style of the garment and the type of fabric.

• Sew two pieces of fabric strips together down the center, wrong sides together. (see Figure 10)

• Press so that the seamline is in the middle of the fabric.

• If using fabric strips, turn under the edges and press. (see Figure 11) If using UltraSuede®, there is no need to turn under a seam allowance.

• Slip the heavy garment seam allowances into the resulting groove and topstitch or catch by hand. (see Figure 12)

Pockets

For many of us, pockets are an absolute necessity. Pockets can be added almost anywhere, in any shape and size. They can be afterthought pockets, add-on pockets, patch pockets, or even faced pockets

Afterthought Pocket

An afterthought pocket is one that you can add to a garment after you have cut the garment pieces out. To create an afterthought pocket: Cut a hand size opening in the side seam where you would like your pocket to be, place a piece of fabric on the wrong side of the garment behind the hole, and topstitch into place (the topstitching becomes a decorative line on the outside of the garment).

Afterthought Pocket

My all-purpose pocket template is on the next page. This is a reduced version of the actual template size but can be enlarged, depending on your hand size, body size and taste. This is the back of the pocket. It is sewn down around the edge to the top garment piece. Shape variations can be made for the pocket opening. After a pleasing shape has been determined, make a pocket facing piece which duplicates the shape of the opening, adding seam allowances and is a width of 2-3".

Place the pocket template opening on the garment to determine pocket placement. When you are happy with the location of the pocket opening, mark the opening shape on the garment. You will need to add your seam allowance to the mark, then cut the opening. Place the facing piece on the garment, right sides together, matching the pocket opening edges, and stitch the facing to the garment. Press, grade and clip the seam. Turn the facing to the inside. Press again. Understitch or topstitch the facing.

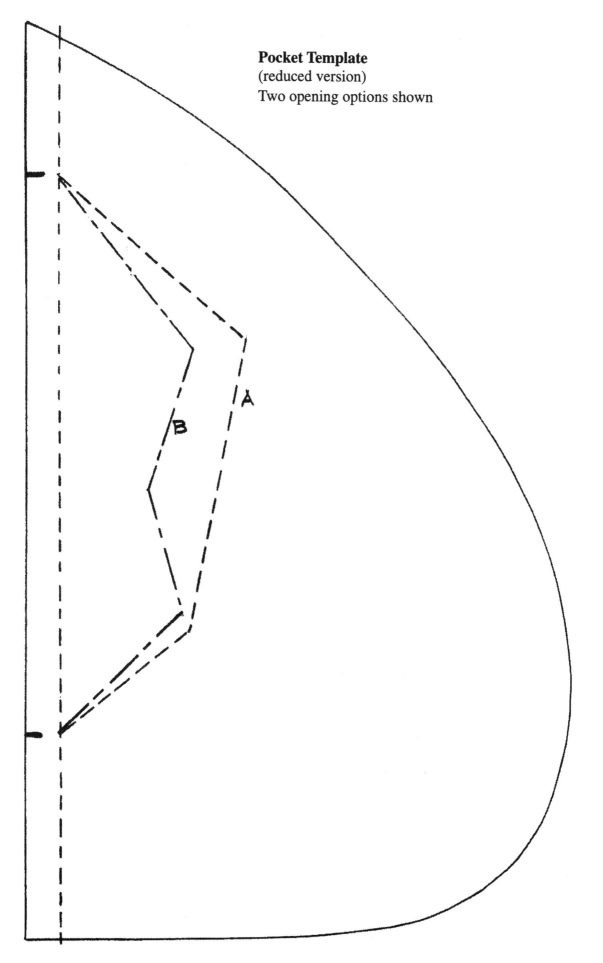

Pocket Template
(reduced version)
Two opening options shown

A

B

Now attach the back pocket and topstitch around the pocket edge. (see Figure 13) If you don't like the look of topstitching on the garment, cut four pockets and use two for facings. These can be made of contrasting or lining fabric. This will also give a cleaner looking pocket.

Add-On Pocket

An add-on pocket is one that is placed in the seam of a jacket, pants or skirt. The following instructions are reprinted with the permission of Gale Grigg Hazen, who has published a number of teaching modules.

Figure 13

Choose any pocket shape and align to match the garment side seam, right sides together. Mark the pocket opening on the garment. Put a 1" × 8" strip of a sheer, stable, sew-in, lightweight interfacing (like Sewin' Sheer), on the right side of the garment, over the area where the pocket opening will be. Using shorter than normal stitch length, sew through the three layers (garment, interfacing, and pocket) from garment edge, in ⅝" at one end of opening. Pivot and sew at ⅝" along the seam allowance, turning at the other end of opening and sewing out to the garment edge. Carefully clip all the way into the corner of both ends. Edgestitch the long edge. Turn inside and topstitch. Trim away excess interfacing. Put right side of pocket to wrong side of garment, pin or glue stick into place. Sewing from wrong side, sew all the way around the pocket. Finish sewing garment, taking special care not to catch the edge of the pocket opening.

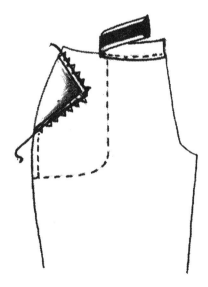

Figure 14

Note: Whether using this pocket or the afterthought pocket for pants, extend the top of the pocket to the waistline seam. (see Figure 14) This anchors it and keeps the pocket from drooping and pulling.

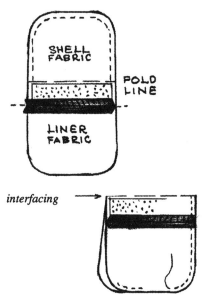

interfacing

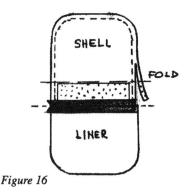

Figure 15

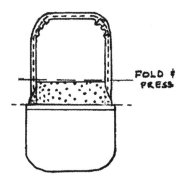

Figure 16

Figure 17

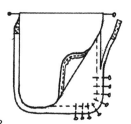

Figure 18

Patch Pocket

The traditional patch usually looks like a rectangle, square or half of an oval. A patch pocket can actually be any shape you choose! When using handwoven fabrics, sometimes all that is left are unconventionally shaped scraps. There is no reason why patch pockets cannot be pieced or the grainline changed. Why not try a triangular or hexagonal shape?

Most patch pockets are topstitched to the garment. This is the easiest method, and especially easy for unconventional shapes. With right sides of lining and pocket together, sew the lining to the pocket, leaving an opening for turning. Press, grade and turn. Place on the garment and topstitch.

The following method allows you how to attach a pocket, with a hand-sewn look, yet have the sturdiness of a topstitched one:

1. With right sides together, sew the pocket lining to the pocket (liner fabric) at the upper edge.

2. Stitch ½" from the side and lower edges through the pocket (shell) only.

3. Press the lining (liner fabric) down and press the top fold line. (see Figure 15)

4. Trim the pocket (shell) seam allowance close to the stitched line. (see Figure 16)

5. Press under the fold line around the pocket edge. (see Figure 17)

6. Place the pocket on the garment where desired (the lining will stick out ⅝" from the pocket).

7. After the pocket placement is determined, pin the lining only to the garment at the fold line at the top of pocket only. (see Figure 18)

8. Using tailor's chalk or a disappearing fabric pencil, trace the outline of the pocket on the lining.

9. Stitch down the pocket facing and lining approximately ¼" in from the marked line. Trim the lining close to the stitching line.

10. Fold down the pocket. It should completely cover the lining.

The pocket can be sewn by hand or anchored with the machine blindhem stitch, keeping the straight portion of the stitching line just outside the pocket. (see Figure 19) On handwoven fabrics, the blindhem stitch becomes almost invisible after pressing. The pocket will not pull out because the machine-sewn lining takes all of the stress.

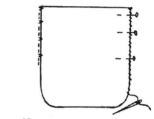

Figure 19

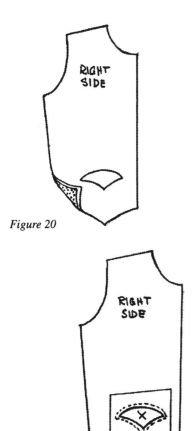
Figure 20

Faced Pocket

Faced pockets are fun and can add a distinctive touch to an otherwise plain garment. Faced pockets can be placed where desired and can be any shape and size. Experiment.

*   Determine the pocket shape and placement and transfer this shape to the garment wrong side. Be sure the pocket area is interfaced. (see Figure 20)

*   Place the lining and garment right sides together. The lining must be large enough for the final shape, but it does not have to be cut to the exact size now. (see Figure 21)

*   Sew the opening shape from the wrong side of the fabric, following your previously marked lines.

*   Cut out the inside of the shape. Press and turn the lining to the garment wrong side. Edgestitch or topstitch the opening window if desired.

*   Place the pocket back over the lining and pin in place. From the front side of the garment, determine and mark the stitching line around the pocket. Avoid a topstitching line by sewing the lining and pocket back layers together, similar to a welt pocket. (see Figure 22)

Figure 21

SUGGESTED SHAPES

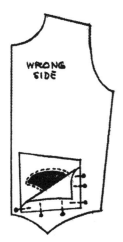
Figure 22

Closures:
Buttons, Buttonholes, Snaps and Waistbands

Buttons

Antique or one-of-a-kind buttons are very appropriate on handwoven garments. If the button is oversized, you may want to sew a small button on the facing side to help support the weight of the button.

Very large buttons can be sewn over a snap or hook-and-loop tape closing.

All functional buttons used on handwoven fabrics need a shank because handwovens are usually bulkier than corresponding commercial fabrics.

Buttonholes

Buttonholes should not be avoided on handwovens, but alternate solutions are sometimes better.

If you choose buttonholes, keyhole buttonholes usually work best. Interface **both** the fabric and the facing. Where the buttonhole is to be placed, interface with an additional patch of interfacing. For fusible interfacing, change the grainline to run perpendicular to the first grainline to give added stability. (see Figure 23)

Use paper over the feed dogs if they grab hairy fibers and do not allow the buttonhole making to proceed smoothly.

Machine buttonholes are cleaner and easier if quilting thread or two strands of regular thread are used in the needle. Use a large-eye needle with a sharp point.

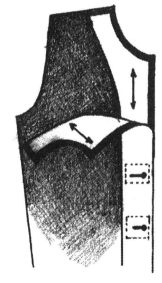

Figure 23

The most critical buttonhole is at the bustline. It should fall between the nipples. Respace as necessary between the neckline top button and the bust, then use the same spacing below the bust.

Buttonhole length is determined by the width and height of the button, plus ⅛" if using a large button or bulky fabric. For odd shaped buttons, the buttonhole must be at least as long as the longest distance from the edge of the button to the shank.

Loop closures may be a better solution to odd-sized or shaped buttons. Measure the length and height of the button to determine the loop length. Lay this length of loop flat along the seamline. Open the seam allowance at the ends only and insert the ends of the loop and restitch. The finished loop will lie flat along the edge and be more secure than loops that form a U.

Snaps

The new decorative snaps can be an attractive alternative to buttons and buttonholes. The small, jewel-tone snaps are delicate enough for lightweight fabrics without tearing the fabric. Large anorak-type snaps work very well for waistbands and bulky fabrics. Make a test closure on a scrap before you choose.

Whatever type of closure you decide upon, interface the area first.

Waistbands

Waistbands are not difficult. And there is no need to use a pattern for one, just follow these simple directions. This waistband looks like a standard tailored waistband, but has built in flex. The inside of the waistband uses an elastic called Ban-rol® Super Stretch XL90 and a small piece of waistband interfacing called Ban-rol® (Original Velvet Smooth Edge). These instructions assume a finished waistband width 1½".

Determine the Waistband Length
Collect these numbers:

Waist length _____

+   Overlap _____
     (overlap of waistband at zipper)

+   2 Seam Allowances _____

Total _____

The total is the cut length of the waistband.

For a 1½" finished width waistband, the cut width of the waistband is 4".

Forming the Waistband
If the overlap is 1" or less, cut ⅛" yard Ban-rol® firm interfacing into two equal pieces. But the Ban-rol® XL90 elastic 1-3" shorter than the waistband (personal preferences rule here, experiment to decide which length you like best). Overlay the small strips of Ban-rol® interfacing on both ends of the elastic and sew securely with a three-step zigzag.

1. Mark the seam allowance on the zipper closure side.

2. Measure the waistband length and make a small, clip in to the seam allowances or mark. Divide the waistband in half and clip or mark again. Divide each half in half and clip or mark. Example: clip center back, two side marks and center front.

3. Pin the waistband to the top of the garment. Each mark should fall on either a side seam or center front or back.

4. Move the waistband side seam marks ¼" towards the front (your waistline is never even, there is always more in the front. If you have a protruding tummy, measure your front and back waist and move the marks accordingly).

5. Sew on the waistband with the skirt or pants against the feed dogs. This helps ease in the excess fabric (and there should be some).

6. Press the seam as sewn. Then press the seamline towards the waistband. Check to see if the waistband width is even at the zipper. If not, deepen or reduce the offending side as necessary.

7. Place the Ban-rol® interfacing and elastic in the waistband.

8. Right sides together, sew the waistband enclosed on the zipper overlap, catching the ends of the Ban-rol® in the ends of the waistband. Clip, press, turn and press.

9. Measure the depth of the waistband from the front side. Continue to measure and pin from the right side. Stitch-in-the-ditch to secure the waistband. The waistband underflap can be zigzagged and trimmed for less bulk.

On bulky handwovens, or any bulky fabric, use a double layer of lining for the backside of the band and interface both sides. Use the feed dogs to advantage by placing the garment down and the waistband facing up.

Speed Tailoring

Speed tailoring is a construction method that provides a clean tailored jacket look, but streamlines many of the steps used in traditional tailoring. The key to speed tailoring is fusible interfacing. To achieve the desired crispness and roll on collars and lapels, different weights of fusible interfacing are fused on top of one another. Test the interfacings on the handwoven fabric for show-through lines and stiffness. Softer is better than stiffer, and for that reason I prefer a fusible knit.

Speed tailoring involves making two separate jackets which are then joined together. One jacket is the lining (complete with sleeves) with the upper collar attached. The other jacket is the fashion fabric with the undercollar attached. The sleeves should be set in both jackets. Complete the sleeves on the outer jacket by hemming and attach the shoulder pads. The process is the same regardless of sleeve and collar style.

The whole front of the outer garment should be interfaced, especially if there are pockets. Without interfacing, pockets will bag and may rip away from your handwoven garment. Interface the back from neckline to just below the shoulder blades (if there are no show-through lines), the facing and both the under- and upper collars, pockets and hem edges. Handwovens will stretch rather than shrink through wear and use.

Follow this step-by-step approach.

1. Fit the pattern, either by pin fitting or making a muslin (and then adjusting the pattern).

2. Cut out all pieces, including the lining and interfacing.

3. Fuse interfacing to all required fabric pieces following the manufacturer's instructions for the proper heat and moisture settings. Use a press cloth and take your time.

4. Sew pockets on jacket fronts, using one of the techniques described in the Pockets Section. It is easier to make or attach pockets on flat garment fronts. Pockets become more difficult to control and place evenly after the shoulder and side seams are sewn together.

5. Sew darts, if included in pattern. Large darts may be a problem on bulkier fabrics. The darts can be divided into two or more or opened and pressed. Bulk can also be reduced by not interfacing the dart area. Horizontal bust darts are pressed up to create a smoother appearance, while vertical darts are pressed toward the garment center.

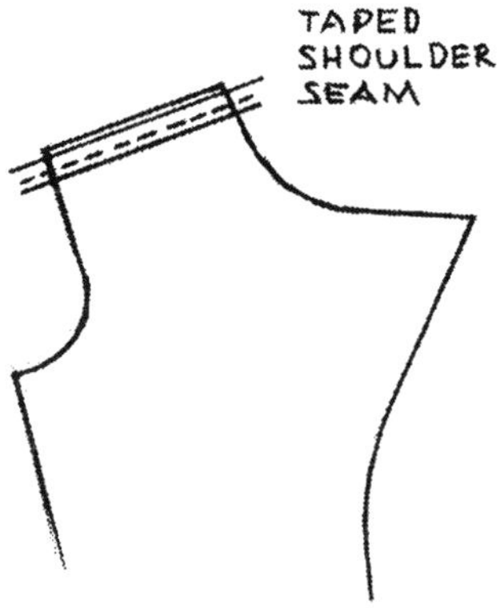

TAPED
SHOULDER
SEAM

Figure 24

6. Sew shoulder seams. Handwovens have more stretch than commercial fabrics so all shoulder seams should have some type of stay for support. My preference is 100%-cotton twill tape for most fabrics. Lightweight fabrics may require linen tape that comes in a variety of widths. For knits and stretchy fabrics, you may prefer to use clear elastic. Whatever you use, the tape gets sewn in the shoulder seam allowance. (see Figure 24) Linen and cotton tapes need to be preshrunk in hot water and allowed to dry. They may be pressed when dry.

7. Baste side seams and fit. Make any needed alterations. After alterations are made, sew the side seams with normal stitch length.

8. Sew underarm seams of sleeves, including sleeve vents if necessary.

9. Set in sleeves. Refer to the Sleeve section for detailed instructions

10. Attach the collar. A good reference for this is Sandra Betzina's *Power Sewing* series. Refer to the next section for different methods to create a roll line on the lapels or undercollar.

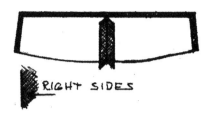

Figure 25

Upper collars and lapels should be larger than their under layers. (see Figure 25) Check to see if this has been added by laying the upper collar pattern piece over the undercollar pattern. The upper collar (and lapel) should form a slight bubble when pinned to their corresponding layers. This extra fabric length is needed for the collar and lapel to roll properly and keep the bottom layer hidden underneath. If both collars are cut the same, it is then necessary to fudge with uneven seam allowances to create enough fabric on top to roll over the edge smoothly. The heavier and bulkier the fabric, the larger the bubble needs to be. Add to the pattern, if needed, by increasing the seam allowance ¼" on the upper layer.

11. Fit the shoulder pads and sew in place, by sewing through the shoulder pad, up through where the two shoulder seams meet. Make this stitch several times. All jackets need shoulder pads. Your body type and the style of the jacket will determine the shape and size.

12. Try on for fit. Make any alterations needed.

13. Hem jacket and sleeves.

14. Construct the inner jacket (lining) as you did the outer jacket.

15. Attach the upper collar to the lining.

16. Sew the two jackets together. Sew all long straight seams first, such as the center front and the unnotched collar edge. Press and grade. Turn, as for the finished seam, and press the rolled edge. Understitch the collar. Turn the garment right sides together again. Wrap the previously sewn seam allowances

to the underside and sew the short seams. It is not necessary to sew right up to the seam on the collar notch. Leave a small hole. This will make the collar and lapel easier to grade and turn. It will also lie flatter after pressing. If the hole is too large or bothersome, use a few hand stitches to close it.

17. After the two jackets are sewn together and all seams have been turned and pressed, stitch the upper and undercollar seam allowances on the body side together at the neckline seam. This is easily done by machine, using a wide zigzag and catching only the neckline seam allowances. This prevents the undercollar from rolling out and keeps the neckline seam secure.

18. Hem the bottom of the sleeve and body lining by hand or use Cecelia Podolak's method of bagging a jacket lining. Leave a pleat for wearing ease.

19. Turn jacket right side out. Do any topstitching required. Complete buttonholes and buttons before giving your garment its final pressing.

Roll Lines

A roll line is where the collar and lapels fold back on themselves.

There are several methods to create a roll line on the lapels or undercollar. These lines are usually marked on the pattern. If they are not, you can determine your own best line during the pattern fitting.

The roll line on a collar determines the stand of the collar (what fits against the nape of the neck). (see Figure 26) The purpose of stabilizing a roll line is to retain memory in the cloth during subsequent use. The roll line should hug the body, not gape or stretch. The lapel roll line keeps your jacket from flaring inward or outward at the center front.

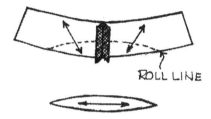

Figure 26

Roll Line Creation -
Collar and Lapel Roll

Fuse a second, slightly heavier, interfacing over the first interfacing layer, using a interfacing such a Pell-Aire® over a fusible tricot in the lapel area and the stand of the collar. Cut the second, heavier piece without seam allowances. Change the grainline to run parallel with the longest edge of the heavier fusible. (see Figure 27)

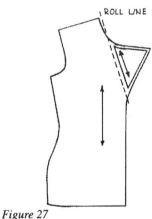

Roll Line Creation -
Lapel Roll, Stay tape method

Fusible stay tape can be used on necklines of any shape to prevent stretching during sewing or wearing. The lapel roll line can be taped with the fusible stay tape placed ¼" from the crease or roll line towards the body of the jacket.

Figure 27

Use the original pattern piece to determine the exact length of the tape. If the garment has stretched so that it is longer than the tape, you will need to shrink the fabric to match the length of the tape. Place the garment on your ironing board, wrong side up. Place the stay tape with the tape ends at the roll line ends. Pin both the garment and the tape to the ironing board. (see Figure 28) Distribute the fullness of the

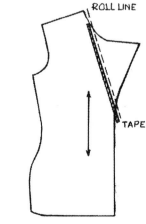

Figure 28

stretched fabric evenly underneath the stay tape. Gently steam the garment and fuse the tape to the garment.

Roll Line Creation -
Lapel Roll, Traditional method
Use traditional machine padstitching with hair canvas to create the roll. This is accomplished by sewing ¼" away from the roll line in the lapel and stand areas. Continue machine stitching rows ¼" apart throughout the area. Do not sew in the seam allowance. The padstitching will show on the underside, but will be covered when the lapel is finished and properly turned. Machine padstitching in the lapel area is commonly used with a twill tape stay line, either machine or hand stitched into place.

Sleeves

Set-in sleeves are not difficult with handwoven fabric. There is usually no need for easing stitches around the sleeve cap, the fabric can be pinned and basted. The underarm of the sleeve should be absolutely parallel with the bodice underarm. Pin this first area, then pin the sleeve cap. There should not be any excess fullness at the top of the sleeve head where it meets the shoulder seam. The sleeve may need to be rotated towards either the front or the back, depending on how your arm hangs. Place the sleeve against the feed dogs to help ease in any excess fabric.

Once the sleeve is inserted satisfactorily, cut a piece of lambswool 3" by 7". Mark it 1" from one lengthwise edge. Center the lambswool at the shoulder seam. Two inches of the 3" side should be placed toward the sleeve with the 1" mark on the seamline. Sew in place with large stitches. This forms the sleeve head and gives a nice rounded appearance to the top of the sleeve. Both edges of the sleeve head and the seam allowance are finger pressed towards the sleeve. Sleeves should hang straight when inserted correctly, not bulge over the upper arm.

Creative Touches

An embellishment is that extra touch, like a pocket, embroidery or a special seam treatment. Do you like to embroider or quilt? Do you have a computerized sewing machine? Or perhaps just a small amount of an extra special yarn or fabric. How about a fabric that would be wonderful except for that one horrid color in it?

Yarn

The simplest embellishments are leftover yarns or even "thrums", which are the left over bits of yarn when the piece is woven. They can be used singly if it is a heavy novelty yarn, or plied. Hold the yarn in place and zigzag over the yarn with matching thread or monofilament thread. (see Figure 29) A metallic or variegated rayon also works well with a decorative stitch to hold the yarn in place.

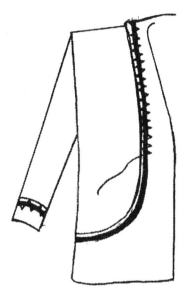

What about that horrible orange thread that detracts from the fabric? Camouflage it with a more attractive thread. If you own a sewing machine with decorative stitches, this is the time to use them. A decorative stitch using metallic thread over a silk yarn is quite distinctive.

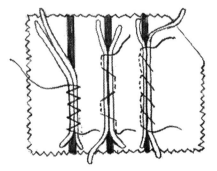

Figure 29
Couch yarns with hand or machine stitching

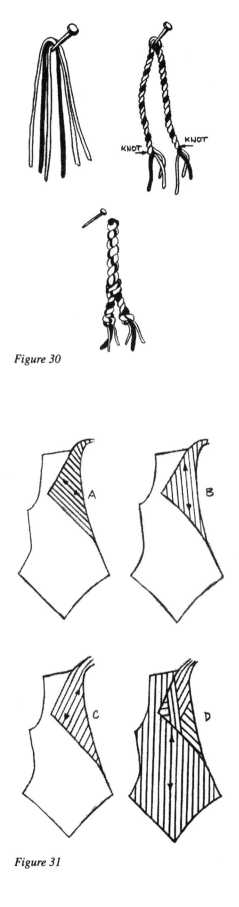

Yarn Twists

Another idea might be to make your own novelty "yarn". Use 4-5 different silk, Ribbon Floss™, metallic or other novelty fiber yarns.

Each yarn length needs to be at least 4 times the finished length. Loop the middle over a stationary object or have someone hold it and start twisting. Twist tightly until the yarns begin to double back on themselves.

At that point, grab the twisted yarn in the middle and hold taut while you put both ends together. Let the middle go and watch the yarn cable upon itself. Secure the ends with an overhand knot. (see Figure 30)

This can now be machine or hand stitched in place. Incorporate the knot and fringe into the design if you like.

Figure 30

Creative Grains

Help! The fabric just isn't large or wide enough unless it's pieced. Usually piecing (adding on a smaller piece to make the fabric longer or wider) is done in the most unobtrusive place. Try a conspicuous place like lapels. (see Figure 31) It then becomes part of the design.

Changing the grainline when piecing also becomes a design detail. Ethnic clothing, using handwoven fabric, often incorporates this detail.

Figure 31

Fringe

Handwoven fabric will usually make a wonderful fringe (unless it is too heavily fulled). Try both the crosswise and lengthwise grain, as they will usually be different. Create a self-fringe on western clothing by inserting a fringed piece of fabric between the yoke and bodice or try a skirt with a fringed hem. (see Figure 32)

Determine the fringe depth. To keep fringe from unraveling, whether it's a garment or table runner, use your blindhem stitch to secure the fringe depth. (see Figure 33) Unravel the fabric to the blindhem stitch by pulling threads out. (Save the threads!) This can go through machine washing and drying and the stitching becomes invisible. If the fringe is uneven, steam or trim it.

Try a plain seam with yarn fringe. The first step is deciding if this should be on the outside or inside of the garment. Sew a plain seam. Using a matching or contrasting yarn, place one strand on the left side, close to the seam allowance. (see Figure 34) Zigzag over it. Do the same on the right side. Now fringe out the seam allowance. The seam has basically been triple stitched and the fringe will not fray.

Try a French seam with fringe. Allow extra width for the seam allowance. Sew the first seam 1", but instead of enclosing the seam allowance for the second seam, let it extend and then fringe it. (see Figure 35)

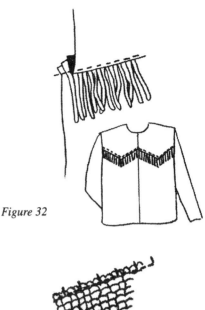

Figure 32

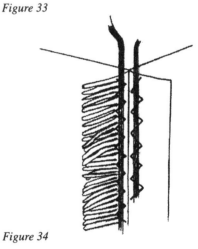

Figure 33

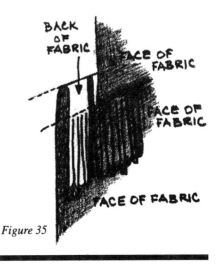

Figure 34

Figure 35

Figure 36

Piping

Piping adds an elegant finish to handwoven and has several advantages when used with handwoven fabric. It provides an attractive edge with several rows of stitching to stabilize loosely-woven fabric. When used on a V-neckline, the piping can also act as a stay to keep the fabric from stretching. Piping does not need to be cut on the bias, especially where it also acts as the stay. The crosswise grain is a good substitute and does have some give.

Piping can also be used as the facing on unlined garments. Make the piping extra wide and tack down by hand or machine. (see Figure 36) This technique also works well for sheer fabrics.

To create and apply piping to a garment:

• Baste the piping using a zipper foot. If your machine has multiple needle positions, now is the place to use them: Set the needle position in from the edge, one or two positions for the initial basting.

• Pin the piping in place and either hand- or machine-baste in place on the garment right side, matching cut edges, stitching on the previous stitching line.

• For the final stitching, layer garment, piping and facing together, position the needle as close to the edge as possible.

Piping can also enhance design lines or help coordinate mixed fabrics. Ethnic styles often use narrow fabric pieces. Extra wide piping with finished edges can cover the seam allowances and unify the design.

Conclusion

Whether you are a sewing enthusiast, weaver or both, I hope this has encouraged your creativity and sparked your enthusiasm for working with handwoven fabrics. They are wonderful to sew and wear. Have fun and enjoy the process as well as the finished garment.

Recommended Reading

(Check your library, bookstore or mail-order source)

Power Sewing
by Sandra Betzina

More Power Sewing
by Sandra Betzina

Flatter Your Figure
by Jan Larkey

The Great Put On
by Lois Ericson

Lessons for EveryBODY
by Gale Grigg Hazen,
The Sewing Place

Easy Guide to Sewing Jackets
by Cecelia Pokolak

Fitting Finesse
by Nancy Zieman

Sources

Fabric
Twill & Tuck
106 N. Washington Avenue
Ritzville, WA 99169
509-659-1913

The Sewing Place
Gale Grigg Hazen
18476 Prospect Avenue
Saratoga, CA 95070
408-252-8444

Mail-order notions; thread; Neue Mode, Stretch & Sew, Lois Ericson's patterns; and books

The Sewing Place
Gale Grigg Hazen
18476 Prospect Avenue
Saratoga, CA 95070
408-252-8444
Website: http://thesewingplace.com

Nancy's Notions
PO Box 683
Beaver Dam, WI 53916
1-800-833-0690
Website: http://www.nancysnotions.com

Clotilde
2 Sew Smart Way
Stevens Point, WI 54481
1-800-772-2891
Website: http://www.clotilde.com

Oregon Tailor's Supply
PO Box 42284
Portland, OR 97242
1-800-678-8457

Pockets

hidden
pocket in
lining between
bust & waist